BEFORE I SELF DESTRUCT

BY LITTLE BLUE

COVER BY SHALINA MITCHELL

TABLE OF CONTENTS

Dedication

I would like to dedicate this book to my city. Philly thank you for creating me and for turning me into a warrior. This book is also dedicated to all of the strong women battling with mental health issues that are progressing and finding new ways to move forward. I would like to dedicate this to the ones who committed suicide, I am sad that you are no longer with us. You will live through me. I dedicate this to my lover, Jaime Lee and to her little wild things. Mommy and daddy this one is for you.

Acknowledgements

A huge thank you to my mentor Francios. You had hope for me and saw the positives even when I couldn't, even after I already gave up on myself. Thank you for saving me. Thank you to Smiley for all of the guidance and for helping me grow into a woman. I appreciate the ones who played a role in me falling apart. I learned a lot from you and the pain was necessary for growth. To my lover, you are my number one fan and I appreciate the love, support and patience you've shown me through my journey. Thank you for positively impacting my mental health and for uplifting my spirit. The universe needs you more than you know. I would like to acknowledge the female creators in Philadelphia. Keep doing your thing and continue to flourish. When you create you are healing others and making my hometown a better place.

Deconstruction

When I succeed,
I want to succeed with you.
Most importantly when I fail,
I want to fail in the presence of you.
I want you to watch me be human.

Out of all the lies
I've heard,
The truth
Is what left
That ringing in my ear.

I have this strange obsession
With picking at a scab
And reopening the wound
I guess that's why
I keep running back to you.

I have this strange obsession
with trying to make a house
Out of playing cards.
I guess that's why I thought
I could create a home in you.

I wear my blackness
Like permanent war paint.
Centuries of royalty
Etched in my skin.
Spiritual hymns
Smoothed out my melanin.

My people ruled kingdoms once.
My people shed blood
On land that they built
From the ground.

My people carried
This country on their backs
With the American flag
Wrapped around their necks.
My people can burn it
Down to the ground
If they wanted to.

I have no choice but to conquer.

My mother named me after a color. Every school year there was someone that asked, "Why did your mom name you that?" I could never answer them because I had the same question. My mother and father don't even know why she chose that name. I hated it, I hated not knowing the reason behind it. So I am on a quest to define my name. To define myself.

The burning
I feel
In my throat
when I say your name,
The sizzle
From the residue
Of you
Stained on my lips
Is the only way I know
That we've ever kissed.
This aching in my heart I feel
Is the only evidence I have
of me ever loving you.
You just left,
And I am forgetting us.

I finally understood why
They give names
To hurricanes
When I started loving you.

It's 2am
And I can't sleep
because I have a poem
Stuck in my esophagus
And I am
Coughing up flowers.

Raw

I like you in the mornings
When you awaken.
Before coffee.
Before make up.
Before the sun gets to you.
Before it breaks
The darkness and sets
the atmosphere ablaze.
Before Seattle's rain
has felt you.
Before work.
Before reality.
Before adulthood.
I like YOU.

Misery is a choice, depression is not. When I learned the difference between depression and misery, I learned control. See when I wake up desolate or feeling like I'm sinking into myself, I create happiness though it takes way more effort and energy. I listen to country, I play guitar, I drink a smoothie, I write down what I am grateful for, I go for a walk. Now I can't help when the darkness comes but I can let some light in. The dark clouds come in but it doesn't have to rain if I don't want it to. I use to tell myself, "I can't get out of bed" but now I tell my body that I will not quit on it, that I choose happiness. This is a choice. Misery is a choice, depression is not.

She began to breathe again.
A natural reaction
due to a lack of oxygen.
The build and collapse
rhythm of the lungs
was normal for everyone else.
Something that was natural at birth,
something that was never taught,
yet she had to learn
the mechanics of breathing again.

I leave roses
In their vase
way past due
Because I think
they are still beautiful.

I need you to tell me
When you fall
out of love with me.
I have a habit of watering
a dying thing.

If Philadelphia Could Talk

Philly would talk about
The vibration of a basketball
Bouncing on the ground.
A staccato heartbeat.
Like a chant.
Like an anthem.

It would whistle
The Fresh Prince theme song
While the corner boys
Bob their heads to it.
Philly made some good music.

Philly would decipher
The tales told
By school girls drawing
Chalk on the sidewalk.

Philly.
Where my grandma
Is your grandma.

Philly.
Where we throw
Block parties
For graduations and celebrations.

Philly.
Where the street lights
Determine when it's time
To go back home.

Philly.
Where we put candles

At street corners for
Our fallen soldiers.
For the brothers that
Didn't go home when
the street lights came on.

There's a hole,
Right here on my left side.
I guess that's a good thing.
I must have been whole
To be able to locate
Where the emptiness is.
I must be whole to have a hole.

-Learning to feel

Your absence lingers
in places
It is not welcomed...
I guess that is called loitering.

I never told my girl
she was like home to me.
Because home for me
was my daddy with
an empty bottle of whiskey.

I found salvation
In starvation.

-Still learning to feel

White cop says, "Hands up."
Black boy listens.
Black boy cries, "Don't shoot."
White cop thinks it's a suggestion.

The number one lesson
I've learned about oppression
Is how quickly my complexion
Can become a death sentence.

I do not know the difference
Between my brown body
And a red target.

And when you hear this
You will sink in your soul
Because you'll know that
This is about you.
I bet you'll wish that I just
Limited you to a haiku.

Aren't All Girls Made of Magic?

After being assaulted,
I did a disappearing act
For days.
And no one noticed
I wasn't the same.

Trust is invisible.
This is how you
Turn it into dust.

This is how you
ugly cry in silence.
This is how you save
Someone's reputation.
This is how you disappear
In broad day light.

This is how you
Carve a smile into
Your face
With no blood
On your hands.

But aren't all girls
made of magic?
Do magicians really
never tell their secrets?

I don't want to be told
that you've never
met anyone like me.
Or I am an anomaly
In your sea.
Tell me that these people do exist.
Tell me that I am not the only one
But then reassure me that
When another wave comes by
To sweep you off your feet
You will not be taken away
By the currents of lust.
Tell me you will always choose me.
Tell me that even through tsunamis
You will stay grounded
And hurricanes are like mist to you.
Say you'll stay.
Show me.

I've been in crowded places and felt
desolate. Been to family events and felt
like a stranger, however I've been in an
empty room with you and felt full. I felt
like I had substance. My favorite thing
about you is your eyes. Not because of the
obvious reason. Not because they are
bluish-grey but because they have a
gravitational pull. Because they see
depths. I can't just say, "I'm okay, I'm
fine," and you just believe it. You call me
out when my energy is off all the time, I
guess that's the indigo child in you huh? I
absolutely love being emotionally naked
with you. Transparency is extremely
important.

God loaned me life, so while I am here I
will be kind. I will breathe life into
others and help uplift. I can't be selfish.
I can't be closed minded, my time here is
limited.

When it rains
It doesn't rain everywhere.
Depression is being on borders.
Borders of rain and sunshine
I'm Borderline of being borderline.

Depression is contradicting.
A black hole so dense,
The more it spreads
The more is makes things empty.

This morning we woke up to each other. I didn't say anything to you, you didn't say anything to me, we didn't need to. We touched. The exchange of energy was a very emotional experience for me. We sat in silence, enjoying each other's warmth and that says so much. Isn't that beautiful? To be so quiet but still love loudly. To really have the world in my hands when I'm holding you. To feel my soul ignite each time my skin meets yours.

The irony of feeling dead
in a living room,
Full of people but feeling alone.
When a house is
No longer a home.

You said we'd take a break
For 3 weeks or so.
I guess this is the "or so" part.

For some reason New Orleans had been calling me spiritually. The most valuable thing I've learned from this experience is that the people here don't care about clothes, there's no competition here. They want to be loved for their art, and their creations. We deserve to be loved raw. Through music, painting, magic, cooking they create love and give love. I've never seen so many black people come together and just share themselves with the world. Thank you NOLA for teaching me this and thank you God for allowing me to learn this with my father. I came for the food and the music and I'm leaving with wisdom that I will hold forever. From the swamps, to the crawfish, to the trombone, NOLA you're amazing. Always know that.

Wandering...
But never lost.

There are no records for
this kind of sadness.
I know because
I've played them all.
There's no poem for
This kind of pain.
I know because I
tried to write it.

I am on a constant metamorphosis,
I am not the same woman
I was this time last year.
I am not the same woman
I was yesterday.
And I will not be the same woman
I am when I dot this period.

"I don't want this part of you"
Which part?
The one where I shut down
each time we speak
on a touchy subject?
Oh wait I know,
you must be talking about
the parts of me
that can't breath
whenever I have an anxiety attack.
Yeah that part of me
falls under the
surface each time.
Or is it just all the subparts
of me that fall under
the category of my depression?
Also known as
the parts that makes
me not good enough
and the parts that
made me go from your
"significant other"
to the inadequate one,
to the person that
can't function in love
(name one person who can).

I want to feel you in
the most intangible ways.
That's how I'll know
I've truly touched you.

Sex opens up a whole other entity. I've never really done it for the physical feeling, but for the enablement of a certain emotional experience. I do it for the moments after, when we just lay restless. Darling you're beautiful. What we do is beautiful. What we create is magical.

I want you to fall into me.
Not collide.
Because with collision,
there's friction and
we're already burnt out.
Fall into me.

I've come back to get my belongings
Oh yeah, and I am taking you with me.

Everyone is going to hurt you.
You are in love,
It's going to hurt.
It is about HOW
They hurt you.

Temptation

When I first saw him
I had no idea that he'd
Hold so much significance to you.
That he'd be the reason
We fell apart.

To the soul I will marry: I'm going to take Polaroid pics of you while you're sleeping because you look peaceful when you're not bitching about how I didn't do the dishes the night before. I want to read what you read so I can know what you know and so we can have discussions about it. On my days off I will blast Elvis Presley. I will hang your paintings all over our house so you know how much I adore your creations. I will hide in the closet with a nerf gun and wait for you to come home from work. On days that you feel unproductive, and uninspired it's okay we can just lay in bed and play sudoku or hang man, as long as your mind is at work. Sandwiches will be cut diagonally. You can have roses if you want but someone wrote that roses always grow in a bunch, they never stand alone...and darling you're much greater than that. I will leave Xmas decor up past Valentine's Day. You will participate in the shenanigans.. oh and I use words like shenanigans. I'll learn your favorite songs on guitar for you but I'll never write you a poem because there are no words to describe my love for you. We will binge watch 90s cartoons. I'll take you to different coffee shops and we can compare the richness of the coffee. And we can have museum dates. We can go on walks on rainy days and kiss in the middle of the street because we're cheesy like that. I'm terrible at making coffee...oh and I'm in love with you, wherever you are.

Don't be like a home for me.
Be like an Asylum
And let me
Marinate in my madness.
Let my demons
Run rapid and cause a ruckus,
Riot with me.
Accept me for my crazy.
Create a home in this chaos.
Accept me.

Walk,
Just walk.
With no destination.

I paid I psychiatrist to insult me
When I could get that for free at home.

I need time to stop.
Just for a little while.
Just so I can
Catch up to it
'Cause everything is
moving on without me
And I am missing the world.

I agree,
I do think it's interesting
how the mind works,
or how the mind
DOESN'T work sometimes.
How in a few moments
you aren't as capable
as you use to be,
how a brain falls apart
and may never
recollect its self.

There was something about her aura
That silenced the riot.
Tamed the beasts in my head,
Settled the seas in my eyes,
Demolished the demons
Hidden in my shadows.

Whatever didn't work out today, take a deep breath it may work out tomorrow with the help of some encouraging words and good energy. Wherever you are in life right now you are doing an excellent job, you and your friends should be so proud of you. Do not worry about how far someone else is in life, you are going at your own wonderful pace. Embrace this moment.

Stop expecting extraordinary actions from extra ordinary people.

Emptiness is a fatal type of full.

Do I think I'll be
going through this forever?
Hopefully, not.
Definitely unpredictable.
Optimistically, no.
Medically, dependent.
Dramatically yes.
Technically, no one lives forever.

"What would you do without me?"
Everything.
I created before you
And I will conquer
After you.
Together we build, construct,
Nourish, teach,
We enhance each other
But you do not make me
Who I am.
Understand?

And the next time you
Utter another obtuse
rhetorical question
Out of those cyanide Lips,
I'll walk away in silence.
And we will see
How much you conquer and create
With that young mind
And flimsy heart of yours.

Being stuck on the future is just as bad as being stuck in the past.

-Anxiety

It's crazy how
we destroyed one another,
How you looked to me to
make you whole again.

How I picked up your pieces
Building you,
not realizing I was
breaking me.

I am done SURVIVING life
I want to start LIVING.

When we got ourselves together,
ticking clocks didn't matter.
It didn't go by fast or slow
time was just time
and we just lived.

                    -Simmering down

Anxiety has been
over welcoming its stay
And it didn't take its
shoes off at the door.
What if it tracks mud in the house?
What if it leaves the door open
And the rain comes in?

Sometimes it leaves its fingerprints
On the medicine cabinet
To remind me that it is still present.
To remind me that
My refill date is approaching.

To remind me that
my body isn't mine.
To remind me that this
Is a forever that I can't escape.

We are running out of time my love.
All of the broken parts of me
Are starting to deteriorate.
And all of the sane
Parts of me have already evaporated.
I wonder how much time I have left
Before the fabricated
Parts of me begin to fade.

Lying on her bed of lies
Was way too comfortable
For me to wake up.

To get the car I wanted I had to stop
buying Jordans for a while, had to stop
going to clubs, had to cook at home instead
of eating out, had to not date for a while
so I can stay focused on my financial
goals. I had to tell myself that my feet
can be fly but I'm gonna be walking to the
bus. Can buy the flyest clothes but gonna
be cold in the winter. It's okay to wear
vans for a while, it's okay to say no and
stay in for the weekend. Save your money
and invest in something more worth it.

I've come back home, only to find that the
people I once shared the same air with
aren't breathing anymore. Some didn't make
it to 21, some of their mothers didn't get
to see them walk across the stage to get
their diploma. Either because they died
before they could or they dropped out. I've
come home to find gum on side walks, trash
in the street and people walking around
homeless men and women on the ground,
because this has become normal. I've lived
in filth my whole little life and didn't
know it. I am so thankful to have moved
past that part of my life because lord
knows I can't raise my son in this mayhem.
Lord knows I can't trust these men with my
daughter when I have one. Lord knows I
couldn't grow anymore and become the woman
I am meant to be while still being here.
Here people don't live, they survive. And
maybe that's honorable but it gets
exhausting. I knew I was growing when I
told myself that I deserved better than
what my city has to offer me. You have to
be so careful here, not stare at anyone for
too long, be home before the street lights
come on, not let anyone know your triumphs.
You'd get killed for rolling your eyes,
looks really do kill. I'm never coming
back.

Hypocrisy

Whether you run to narcotics
Or run towards Christ
You are still running.
Let's face it
Neither of us truly faced it.

The Hood

I'm glad I've had certain experiences in the hood, the only thing I hate was not having my family by my side to defend me...but it all helped me grow into a woman. I'm prepared for the world, for internal and external wars. I'm just not prepared for love. The hood don't teach you how to do that part.

To fully understand the
construction of something
You must dismantle it to
The core
And be conscious of
The order you disassembled
It in.

I have a strange love for
How objects were built
So I decided to take myself
Apart, for you.
I decided to unfold for you.
And I lost some tiny
But crucial pieces.
And now I may never be whole again.

This day is always so confusing for me. I honestly don't know what it's like to have a mother and I don't ever talk about it but I guess I'll write about it. My mother has schizophrenia, so we never really had a chance to have that whole mother-daughter thing. She wasn't/isn't like other moms. She sees things, hears voices, has trouble taking care of herself but I refused to call her crazy. I loved her too hard to believe that something was wrong. Her brain was so occupied on other things that she couldn't be my mother. We had some good moments together when I was a child, very few moments but I do remember. And before she went completely "crazy" she was highly intelligent and had a good heart but for the most part I didn't have a mom. I use to look in her eyes and search for THAT love. The love only a mother could give but she was so distant, right next to me but distant. She never hugged me, there were only a few occasions she told me she loved me but I doubt she meant it. I don't think she's capable of loving but I guess she would if she could. I just missed out on so much and I can't get my childhood back. I can't go back and have those mommy-daughter talks. I don't even know what a mommy-daughter talk is but I know I needed them. I'm doing great but I wish she gave me some guidance. We never got our toes done, we never talked about my responsibilities for when I become a wife, she never taught me what people I should watch out for, or whatever other things mommies do with their

daughters. I never had that. She missed
several holidays because she was either in
prison or the crazy house. Never showed up
to a soccer game or a parent teacher
conference...I'm going to stop writing
because it's setting in.

                                    -Mother's Day

She liked puzzles
But she never finished them.
She always left them
all over the place.
All disassembled
All scattered
All dispersed.

She couldn't figure us out.

Don't say that I
Never wanted you like this.
Say you didn't realize it.
Say you were too caught up
in other things
to notice that your woman
absolutely adored you.

Excuse me,
I apologize
If I am loving you
the wrong way
But I am broken.
And trying to figure out
How to love myself
Completely when I was
never whole
To start with.
So I had to love
you in fragments.
I guess that's why we
were never fulfilled.

I don't have moments.
I have days, and decades.
These feelings last for
What seems like forever.

What a blessing it is to be 22 and not in the system. To be 22 and not be a statistic. Man 21 had its highs and lows. 21 was letting go of bitterness and welcoming forgiveness. 21 was buying my 1st car then totaling it. It was adaptation; letting go of my hood mannerisms and learning to be calm. It was understanding that I deserve love. 21 was feeling deeply about temporary mofos. I don't have who/ what I started with but what I DO have is the understanding that I can push forward no matter the set back. I just thank God for allowing me to walk into 22 with valuable lessons learned and with a heart that still loves. 22 will be a hot mess lmao but I'll kick ass like I always do.

Real Talk

I want to give you something raw. Here are some text messages that I've sent to people.

Don't ever think that your art is not
acceptable because it's too depressing. I
rather have your depressing art hanging up
on my wall than some fake happy shit.

-12:57

Says your essence. Says your smile. Says
your poems. Says your paintings. Says your
passion. Says your patience. Says your
commitment. Says your soul.

-18:42

I just wish I had her for a little longer
that's all. It was in God's plan for her to
be mentally ill but I just needed more
time.

-05:10

                              Missing my mother

Awww that's very sweet my darling. I love you too. There are so many things I am confused about, it sucks being in my 20s not knowing what direction to go in. Not knowing if I should eat tacos or salmon lol so many hard decisions. But the one thing I don't need guidance on is loving YOU.

-16:38

I think depression will continue to come
and go but we will learn to keep it away
for longer durations.

-08:40

You are very rare, don't let anyone steal your magic. I pray that if your light ever dims that you will ignite even brighter. Don't let your past hinder you from being successful and seeing your true beauty.

-15:24

I love you more, and I'll take care of you
on days you feel like a dying flower. I'll
save you every time. I'll go after you when
you are lost, when you are drowning.

-21:05

We never try to change algorithms, we never put puzzle pieces where they don't fit. So I'm not going to interrupt your character from being itself.

-10:50

Our story is my favorite, it's so simple.
Us enjoying each other in a parking lot.
How wonderful is that? I don't need a
Hollywood love story, simplicity is
beautiful. No "I took you to a carnival and
won you a stuffed animal." Just me, you and
a good vibe.

-09:59

At some point you did really love me. But I
noticed when you didn't love me as much, a
real woman always knows. I just didn't say
anything. The sex was different, it wasn't
as gentle. You became different.

-11:41

But seriously, when you're down text/call
me. You don't even have to tell me you're
sad. We can laugh and pretend everything is
going right, we can count stars, we can
talk about what causes volcanoes to erupt,
we can talk about how life would be if we
were mermaids. idc just talk to me.

-00:13

I've had several people put their hands on
me and I've been cheated on and left
behind. I'm not use to someone really
wanting me. So I have some issues with self
worth. But that is my problem, not yours.
I'm sorry for bothering you.

-18:10

People loving you BUT not showing it is
almost equivalent to NOT loving the person.
Y'all out here trying to love with hollow
hearts.

-23:20

I got more than your back. I got your spine
when you can't walk, I got your respiratory
system when you can't breathe, I got your
shattered pieces when you fall a part, I
got your teeth and tongue when you can't
form words to express yourself. I got you
homie.

-22:09

I thank you for every time you sent me a message early in the morning so I can wake up to something beautiful. I thank you for any time that you've prayed for me and asked God to watch over me and give me the strength to continue on. I thank you for laughs we shared at 3am. I thank you for each time you told me to have a good day, I thank you for thinking of me during the day. I thank you for being a role model and showing me that wonderful people do exist. You're a magnificent man. I appreciate you.

-19:48

I try to use my page to encourage others because so many of my brothers and sisters are hurting and I hate to watch them bleed. People have become so accustomed to pain they don't even know they are hurting. So many of my people are lost and I just want to give guidance. It hurts seeing people with potential fall. Once I saw this issue, it became my responsibility.

-07:44

Do you still love me? lol I have to double
check every once in a while

-12:44

Understand, I love you but I do NOT need
you. And you don't need me. You are a
wonderful addition to my life. But that is
what you are, an addition. Meaning Though I
am amazing with you I will be more than
fine without you.

-11:14

Good Morning.. I'll be honest, my
depression came back and there's a lot
going on for me right now. I will not be
able to return to work. I'm sorry, I know
how this effects the whole store. I really
am sorry. But it's hard for me to smile and
perform my job with so many things on my
mind.

-10:25

You do "human" so well.

-12:08

I don't want to build you, I want to give
you the supplies and YOU build yourself. So
at the end you can say, " I did this."

-10:21

How many cigarettes did you smoke?

-21:17

Just letting you know that I am thinking of you and I have not forgotten about you. I am concerned and I do care , I hope you are taking care of yourself.

-06:13

Positivity looks so beautiful on. And I
never want to undress these parts of you.
You look amazing clothed in optimism.

-09:30

Tell me what's wrong, open up to me. It's safe.

-18:00

I don't really know what gentle is like. So
I won't know how to behave when being
treated with care.

-10:09

I remember that day. My mom got me up early
to go to court with her. My mom and dad
were fighting for custody over me and then
my mom got too hype and rowdy with the
judge and she got locked up that day..
again. I remember them putting her in cuffs
and I remember hearing the judge grant my
dad full custody of me. I walked in with my
mom and walked out with my dad.

-09:14

And the great thing about it is, when I removed her from my life it wasn't out of anger, regret, fear, pettiness, or confusion. However it was out of security, peace, illumination and the desire to have better for myself.

-12:18

Not all endings are bad my love. And of
course we won't get better but that's only
because you said so and because you spoke
it into existence, create your own truth
darling. Have faith in us.

-19:44

To answer your question, that is what my intentions are. My intentions are to be a good person to you, help you evolve, be whatever is missing in your life. My intentions are to encourage you and introduce you to new experiences and bring out some great qualities that you never even knew you had.

-16:10

Self love

That is greater than any love I could ever
share with another human being.

-11:25

I don't think we really go anywhere after
death. I think we stay here, and just
become something else. Maybe we become a
tree or a plant. Maybe we transfer into a
new born's body. Maybe we will become
electricity or a music note.

-11:07

Maybe your eyes are just seeing the bad.
You have to train them to see the good, you
have to start counting your blessings.

-13:05

But she's unhappy so she doesn't know how
to radiate happiness. Don't let someone who
feels low make you feel low.

-12:53

I've been there. Millions of times. I was
not scared of death.. but I was scared of
not leaving anything behind. If I die now I
wouldn't have a legacy, music, poems, none
of that. I wouldn't leave ANYTHING behind
and that is what scared me. The world isn't
done with me yet and I am not done with the
universe. I WILL not leave this world
without publishing my book, having a baby,
etc. There are poems for me to write, and
an aisle to walk down.

-20:26

I think this is called happiness...I'm not
sure.

-17:12

I know. But there's something about a
certain type of silence that speaks
volumes.

-11:52

I'm not use to love being this kind,
patient or gentle. I've never had a
reassuring love like this before...it
scares me.

-10:57

You're a coward. You fought me but you
never fought for me, you never fought for
us and what we built. You let another woman
take me from you and you just watched. You
felt me slip from your grip unhurriedly and
you allowed it to happen. I wanted you to
fight for me...You are a coward.

                              -never delivered

I trusted you. ME. I trust no one. But I trusted you, and not only did I trust your words but I trusted your character. I trusted that you wouldn't do that with a guy like HIM and wouldn't do that to a woman like ME. I trusted you. I could never trust you again.

-18:48

I think that's beautiful though. A true
artist puts their raw selves into their
art. You were sad so that was your style. I
wouldn't want you to only paint happy
pictures because in reality, life is not
always pretty. This shit isn't pretty at
all. It's not a mistake to portray your
dark thoughts in your paintings. It's bold,
it's honest, it's true, it is beautiful.

-13:25

Good poetry is supposed to make you feel
something. Whether it's happiness, guilt,
hate, peace, sympathy, pathetic, ambitious.
When reading a good poem you should FEEL.
And your poems shook me, I felt my bones
ache.

-21:48

I get like this. I get numb and lifeless
and dead inside. Like I'm in the experience
but I am not actually experiencing. I hate
when everything around me is in motion and
I'm just.. idk This is just one of those
nights.

-01:34

I will change your views on love again. I
promise. Even if it's just me being an
amazing friend and loving you
unconditionally. I've been there. I've
hated love before, not too long ago. I've
hated love a few times in my life and then
forgave it as well. This is a part of life.

-11:57

Dandelions are overlooked, people call them "weeds" as if they are not worthy enough to be called an actual flower. They hold so much significance. Dandelions make me SO happy! And I love but hate the whole concept of making a wish and blowing on them. It's like people just use them to get what they want and then toss it to the side when they are no longer beautiful or when they can't benefit from them anymore.

-11:40

Yes I agree, you can tell a lot about a
person by their art and it absolutely means
the world when someone actually shares
their art with you. I mean really SHARE
their art. Explaining to them every detail,
letting them in on every secret of each
line of a poem or the secret behind each
paint stroke, etc. People really put
themselves into their art. My spirit, my
fears, my happiness, my doubts, my trust,
my soul lies in between the lines of my
art.

-16:47

Made in the USA
Monee, IL
17 July 2020

36658649R10079